THE CIVIL WAR AND RECONSTRUCTION
REBELLION AND REBUILDING

THE CAVALRY IN THE CIVIL WAR

COMPILED BY JOANNE RANDOLPH

PowerKiDS press.

Published in 2018 by The Rosen Publishing Group, Inc.
29 East 21st Street, New York, NY 10010

"The Cavalry Earns Its Spurs" by Philip L. Bolté from Cobblestone Magazine (December 2002).
"Confederate Cavalry Leaders" by Jerry Miller from Cobblestone Magazine (December 2002).
"Union Cavalry Leaders" by Jerry Miller from Cobblestone Magazine (December 2002).

Cataloging-in-Publication Data

Names: Randolph, Joanne.
Title: The cavalry in the Civil War / compiled by Joanne Randolph.
Description: New York : PowerKids Press, 2018. | Series: The Civil War and Reconstruction: rebellion and rebuilding | Includes glossary and index.
Identifiers: LCCN ISBN 9781538340868 (pbk.) | ISBN 9781538340851 (library bound) | ISBN 9781538340875 (6 pack)
Subjects: LCSH: United States. Army. Cavalry--History--Civil War, 1861-1865--Juvenile literature. | United States--History--Civil War, 1861-1865--Cavalry operations--Juvenile literature.
Classification: LCC E492.5 C358 2018 | DDC 973.7'4--dc23

Designer: Katelyn E. Reynolds
Editor: Joanne Randolph

Photo credits: Cvr, p. 1 Stock Montage/Stock Montage/Getty Images; cvr, pp. 1–32 (background texture) javarman/Shutterstock.com; cvr, pp. 1–32 (flags) cybrain/Shutterstock.com; cvr, pp. 1–32 (scroll) Seregam/Shutterstock.com; pp. 5, 8, 14, 15, 16, 18, 19, 20, 21, 23, 24, 26, 27, 28, 29 courtesy of the Library of Congress; p. 6 Google Art Project/Art Gallery of New South Wales/Wikipedia.org; p. 10 Júlio Reis/Tintazul/Wikipedia.org; p. 12 National Archives and Records Administration, cataloged under the National Archives Identifier (NAID) 518135 (https://catalog.archives.gov/id/518135)/Wikipedia.org.

Manufactured in the United States of America

CPSIA Compliance Information: Batch #CS18PK: For Further Information contact Rosen Publishing, New York, New York at 1-800-237-9932

CONTENTS

WORDS IN THE GLOSSARY APPEAR IN **BOLD** TYPE THE FIRST TIME THEY ARE USED IN THE TEXT.

THE CAVALRY EARNS ITS SPURS

In America, **cavalry** came of age in the Civil War. It played a part in one of the first significant battles of that war—the First Battle of Manassas (also known as Bull Run) in 1861. **Confederate** colonel J.E.B. Stuart led five hundred troopers against a **Union infantry** (foot soldiers) **regiment**. Striking the Northern column, the cavalry dealt a heavy blow to the enemy. And in one of the last actions of the war in March 1865, Union major general James Wilson invaded Alabama with almost fifteen thousand cavalrymen. So, the cavalry performed important duties for both sides during the Civil War and matured as a force to be reckoned with in combat.

The First Battle of Bull Run, depicted here, took place on July 21, 1861.

This painting shows a cavalry charge led by Napoleon I in 1807. It is a good example of how cavalry went into battle.

By the eighteenth century, cavalry units in Europe had developed into an important part of every major army. They usually made up about twenty-five percent of an entire force. In America, however, cavalry was virtually unknown. This was mainly because its use was impractical in the mostly wooded terrain of the colonies. Even during the Revolutionary War, although **militia** and Continental army cavalry units were employed, major battles were fought by infantry and **artillery**. And cavalry played only a minor role in the War of 1812.

In the early 1800s, militia on horseback often helped protect American settlers from Native Americans. But it was not until major westward expansion into the Northwest and Louisiana territories that the U.S. Congress recognized the need for a mounted force to protect Americans moving west. In 1833, the Regiment of **Dragoons** was formed. It was trained to fight on horseback or on foot. After another regiment was organized in 1836, the two units were designated First and Second Dragoons.

This image, created around 1847, shows U.S. dragoons in battle during the Mexican-American War.

In 1846, after the start of the Mexican-American War, a third mounted regiment was developed to help establish a military road to the Oregon **Territory**. Called the Regiment of Mounted Riflemen, it ended up going south to join the invasion force at Vera Cruz, Mexico. The Second Dragoons participated in every battle of that war, while the First secured New Mexico and California for the United States.

The years between 1848 and 1860 saw the U.S. Army involved in a series of marches, expeditions, and **campaigns** against Native Americans. The Army protected settlers' wagon trains and explored and mapped the western territory. With the United States expanding, the regiments of the Army were scattered, mostly in the west and southwest.

In 1855, Congress recognized the need for more mounted troops and added two new regiments, called the 1st and 2nd Cavalry. They were created to cover the great distances on the frontier and to deal with the talented horsemanship of the Plains Indians.

This map shows the Union and Confederate states in 1864, during the Civil War.

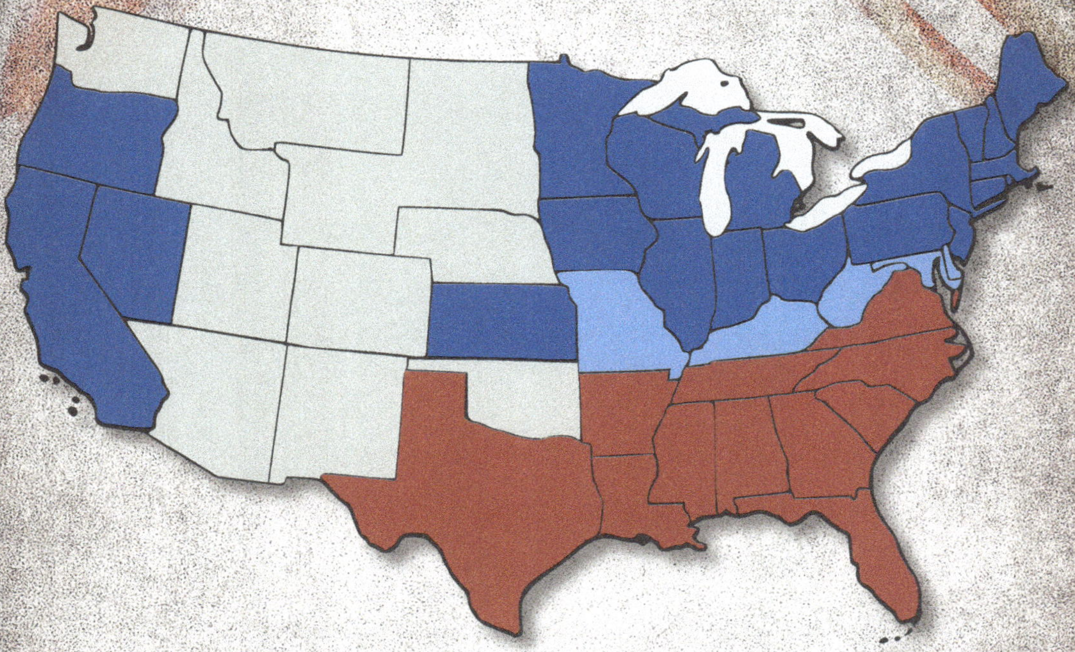

- Union states
- Union states that permitted slavery
- Confederate states
- Territories

When Southern states began to **secede** from the Union and the Civil War began in 1861, many army officers remained loyal to their states. Most Southern officers resigned from the U.S. Army and joined the Confederate army. This included four of the five colonels in command of the existing horse regiments.

In 1861, the 3rd Cavalry was added to the Army. Shortly thereafter, the six mounted regiments were renamed 1st through 6th Cavalry. Their numbers were based on their dates of establishment.

All these regiments served throughout the course of the Civil War for the Union. At first, Union leaders were not enthusiastic about having mounted units. The land did not favor their use, the units were expensive to equip and maintain, and they took a long time to train. Besides, officials believed the war would be over quickly. It was not until early 1862—a year into the war—that the North identified its need for more cavalry.

General J.E.B. Stuart was well known and well respected for his skilled leadership of cavalry in the Confederacy's offensive operations.

In the South, on the other hand, the value of cavalry was recognized early. Most young men knew how to ride, and many already belonged to mounted militia units. Confederate leaders saw the potential usefulness of large cavalry forces. They raised many volunteer cavalry regiments from every state. By 1862, Confederate brigadier general J.E.B. Stuart (he was promoted in September 1861) already was commanding all of the cavalry of General Robert E. Lee's Army of Northern Virginia. But it was the spring of 1863 before Union brigadier general Joseph Hooker brought the cavalry of the Army of the Potomac under a single commander.

So, during the first half of the war, Southern cavalrymen almost always were victorious over their Northern counterparts. But by the summer of 1863, the Confederate cavalry was encountering large losses of men, as well as a lack of horses and good **forage**. The Union cavalry, meanwhile, improved in effectiveness and overall quality, and added numbers of state volunteer regiments. The benefits of the cavalry for both sides were proven time and again.

CONFEDERATE CAVALRY LEADERS

Virginian Turner Ashby had no military experience before the Civil War, but he quickly became Major General Stonewall Jackson's best-known cavalry leader. The personal courage Ashby displayed in the Shenandoah Valley campaign was admired by both Union and Confederate soldiers. His magnificent horsemanship and daring raids made Ashby the Civil War's first cavalry legend. His major weakness was his lack of skill in gathering information. Despite the fact that Jackson did not support his promotion, Ashby was made a brigadier general in May 1862. He was killed in a skirmish just one year after the war began.

TURNER ASHBY

Nathan Bedford Forrest of Tennessee was considered by many to be the most brilliant cavalry leader of the war. Very poor and not well educated as a boy, Forrest became a wealthy businessman and slave trader. He joined the Confederate army at the age of forty. Even with no military experience or training, Forrest was nicknamed "the Wizard of the Saddle" and gained a promotion to brigadier general in less than a year. During the Civil War, twenty-nine horses were killed from under him in battle. Forrest also killed thirty soldiers in close combat—an amazing record for a general. Fighting mostly in the West—Mississippi and Tennessee—Forrest was the only soldier on either side to rise in rank from private to lieutenant general.

NATHAN BEDFORD FORREST

Wade Hampton had initially opposed the division of the Union, but remained loyal to his state of South Carolina when it became the first state to secede.

Thomas Green moved to Texas from Tennessee in 1835, fought in the war for Texas's independence from Mexico, and later served in the U.S.-Mexican War. He led cavalry units in every trans-Mississippi battle that involved the Texas cavalry in the Civil War. During the Red River Campaign in Louisiana, Green led cavalry attacks against several Union gunboats that had run aground. He was killed by a shell fired from one of the boats.

Wade Hampton was born to wealthy parents on a South Carolina **plantation**. When the Civil War broke out, he was forty-three years old, owned 3,000 slaves, and was one of the richest men in the South. Although he had no military experience, Hampton became an exceptional leader and rose to the second-highest rank in the Southern army. He was given his first cavalry command under Brigadier General J.E.B. Stuart and participated in Stuart's ride around the Union army in Maryland. Hampton also fought at Antietam, Fredericksburg, Gettysburg, the Wilderness, and Petersburg. Upon Stuart's death, Hampton took his place and proceeded to perform brilliantly as General Robert E. Lee's cavalry commander. After the war, Hampton became South Carolina's governor and later a U.S. senator.

John Hunt Morgan joined the Confederate army even though his home state, Kentucky, remained loyal to the Union. He soon was promoted to command of the 2nd Kentucky Cavalry. Morgan's daring raids in Tennessee, Kentucky, Ohio, and Indiana made him a legend. While leading the longest cavalry raid of the war—600 miles through Union territory into southern Ohio—Morgan was defeated and captured. Four months later, he and six of his officers carried out a daring escape from the Ohio State Penitentiary. In 1864, Union cavalrymen killed Morgan during a raid on his Tennessee headquarters.

JOHN HUNT MORGAN

A graduate of West Point, J.E.B. (James Ewell Brown) Stuart fought with the U.S. Cavalry in Kansas against the Cheyenne Indians and pursued the abolitionist **guerilla** leader John Brown before the Civil War. In the first major battle of that war, Stuart's cavalry charge helped turn Manassas into a Confederate victory. He was promoted quickly to commander of cavalry for the Army of Northern Virginia. In 1862, Stuart led 1,200 cavalrymen on a reconnaissance behind enemy lines. Riding entirely around Union major general George McClellan's army, Stuart lost only one soldier. This "Ride Around McClellan" was hailed as one of the greatest cavalry exploits of all time. Stuart's success in collecting accurate information through intelligence-gathering methods was extraordinary. He also fought at Seven Days, Second Manassas, Antietam, Fredericksburg, Chancellorsville, Brandy Station, Gettysburg, and the Wilderness. Stuart was killed at the Battle of Yellow Tavern in 1864.

STUART'S RIDE AROUND McCLELLAN

Another West Point graduate, Earl Van Dorn, served with distinction in the Mexican-American War. His service in Texas during the early days of the Civil War led to his promotion to commander of the Army of the Mississippi. Unfortunately, Van Dorn was a failure in that position and lost two major battles. After being replaced by Lieutenant General John C. Pemberton, Van Dorn redeemed himself through his brilliant leadership of Pemberton's cavalry. In 1862, he led a successful cavalry raid on the supply depot at Holly Springs, Mississippi. This forced Union major general Ulysses S. Grant to abandon his first Vicksburg campaign.

EARL VAN DORN

Joseph Wheeler graduated from West Point in 1859 and fought with the Regiment of Mounted Riflemen against the Apache Indians. After serving courageously at Shiloh, he was given command of the Army of Mississippi's cavalry. Wheeler fought at Chickamauga and Chattanooga and led one of the most important cavalry raids of the Civil War in Tennessee. Wheeler showed his heroism by slowing down Union major general William T. Sherman's march through Georgia. All together, "Fighting Joe," as he was nicknamed, participated in 200 Civil War engagements and 800 skirmishes. After the war, he served in the U.S. House of Representatives for Alabama. Wheeler returned to military service during the Spanish-American War and led the U.S. Cavalry forces in Cuba.

JOSEPH WHEELER

UNION CAVALRY LEADERS

Kentuckian John Buford graduated from West Point in 1848 and served on the frontier as a captain in the Second Dragoons. During the early part of the Civil War, Buford was a staff officer in Washington, D.C. He did not see combat until the Battle of Second Manassas in August 1862. Buford was wounded so badly there that an erroneous announcement was made of his death. His most remarkable accomplishment came at Gettysburg. There, Buford opposed the initial Confederate attack and managed to hold off forces much larger than his own until the rest of the Union army could organize for battle. Buford's heroic stand probably prevented a Union disaster. After fighting in numerous engagements during the Rappahannock Campaign in Virginia, Buford fell ill. He died in December 1863. His promotion to major general was made official on his deathbed.

John Buford's heroic leadership of his troops during the battle of Gettysburg contributed to the Union's victory there.

Today, George Armstrong Custer is best remembered for his stunning defeat at the Battle of the Little Bighorn in 1876.

George Armstrong Custer, an Ohio blacksmith's son, graduated from West Point just as the Civil War began. With his long hair, fancy uniforms, and love of publicity, he was probably the most **flamboyant** of the Union cavalrymen. At the age of 23, Custer became the leader of the Michigan cavalry brigade and the youngest general in the Union army. He served with distinction at Gettysburg and turned out to be Major General Philip Sheridan's most trusted and reliable cavalry leader in the Shenandoah Valley campaign of 1864. Custer's pursuit of Confederate general Robert E. Lee's retreating army in 1865 helped bring about Lee's surrender at Appomattox Court House.

After the Civil War, Custer fought in the Indian Wars until his death at the Battle of the Little Bighorn. Much of Custer's reputation today is based on his campaigns against Native Americans. Ironically, he also risked his career to fight against government corruption in the Indian Bureau (which had been set up to assist American Indians).

Judson Kilpatrick, a New Jersey farmer's son, graduated from West Point in 1861. He was given command of a Union cavalry regiment that same year. From that time until his transfer to Major General William T. Sherman's command in 1864, Kilpatrick fought in almost every major engagement involving the Army of the Potomac's cavalry. Despite many military successes, however, Kilpatrick was a controversial figure. He often was accused of being a reckless braggart, as well as not entirely truthful in describing his battle exploits. In addition, Kilpatrick earned the nickname "Kill-Cavalry" because of the poor care he took of his men and horses. Nevertheless, he was Sherman's personal choice as cavalry commander on the "March to the Sea," a role he carried out with distinction. Kilpatrick later became active in politics, serving twice as U.S. minister to Chile.

JUDSON KILPATRICK

Born in Washington, D.C., Alfred Pleasonton graduated from West Point in 1844. He fought in the Mexican-American War and later against the Seminole and Sioux Indians. At the outbreak of the Civil War, the cavalry regiment Pleasonton commanded rode its horses from Utah to its new station in Washington, D.C. Pleasonton served with the Army of the Potomac's cavalry in numerous battles and led the Union forces at Brandy Station, the largest all-cavalry battle of the war. After Gettysburg, Major General Ulysses S. Grant removed Pleasonton from command of the Army of the Potomac's cavalry and transferred him to Missouri to fight in the western theater. Pleasonton was a sound, but not brilliant, commander. He retired from the army in 1866 and later worked for the Internal Revenue Service.

ALFRED PLEASONTON

West Point graduate Philip Sheridan spent the first year of the Civil War as a supply officer. Given a cavalry regiment to command, he soon defeated a Confederate force that greatly outnumbered his own at Booneville. That action won him a promotion to brigadier general. Grant appointed Sheridan to be Pleasonton's replacement as chief of cavalry for the Army of the Potomac in March 1864. Sheridan taught Union commanders how to turn the cavalry into a devastating force. Given leadership command of the Army of the Shenandoah, Sheridan continued to use his cavalry units more effectively than other Union commanders. After he drove the Confederates from the Shenandoah Valley, Sheridan took command of Grant's cavalry, relentlessly pursuing Lee's army

Philip Sheridan

until its surrender at Appomattox Court House. Nicknamed "Little Phil" because he stood just five feet five inches tall, Sheridan remained in the U.S. Army after the Civil War, becoming its commanding general in 1884.

James Wilson of Illinois graduated from West Point in 1860. When the Civil War began, he served as an engineering officer until being appointed chief of the Cavalry Bureau. There, Wilson, whose responsibility it was to choose cavalry equipment, made the wise decision to adopt the Spencer repeating carbine rifle. This weapon greatly increased the Union cavalry's firepower. Wilson then requested and received command of a cavalry division, where he proved himself an outstanding combat leader. In the closing days of the war, Wilson carried out a long and very successful independent cavalry campaign. It included a crushing defeat of outnumbered Confederate cavalryman Nathan Bedford Forrest and ended with the capture of Jefferson Davis, president of the Confederacy. After the war, Wilson built and managed railroads. In 1898, he returned to military duty during the Spanish-American War.

JAMES WILSON

GLOSSARY

artillery: Cannon and other large-caliber guns.

campaign: A series of military actions that are designed to achieve a certain purpose, usually in a certain area or using a particular kind of fighting.

cavalry: Soldiers who fight on horseback.

Confederate: Joined by treaty or agreement. The Confederacy was a group of states that joined together to form their own country and separate from the United States.

dragoons: Well-armed troopers in some European armies during the 17th and 18th centuries who were trained to fight mounted or dismounted.

flamboyant: Given to showy displays.

forage: Food for animals.

guerilla: A member of a small, irregular military band that operates by way of surprise attacks on the enemy.

infantry: Soldiers that fight on foot.

militia: An army composed of ordinary citizens rather than trained professionals.

plantation: An estate on which crops such as tobacco, sugar, and coffee are grown by resident workers.

regiment: A permanent unit of an army that is often under the control of a colonel and may be subdivided into several smaller squadrons or units.

secede: To withdraw formally from a federal, political, or religious alliance.

territory: An organized area of a country that is not yet given the full rights of a state.

Union: An organized group formed by people with a common interest. In the Civil War, the Union referred to the United States and those states that remained part of the Union, rather than seceding.

FOR MORE INFORMATION

BOOKS

Lasseur, Allison. *At Battle in the Civil War: An Interactive Battlefield Adventure*. Mankato, MN: Capstone Press, 2015.

Link, Theodore. *George Armstrong Custer: General of the U.S. Cavalry*. New York: Rosen Publishing, 2003.

Uschan, Michael V. *Cavalry During the Civil War*. Farmington Hills, MI: Lucent Press, 2002.

WEBSITES

Introduction to Civil War Cavalry
https://ehistory.osu.edu/exhibitions/Regimental/cavalry

Cavalry
http://www.civilwar.com/overview/315-weapons/148532-cavalry-62478.html

Publisher's note to educators and parents: Our editors have carefully reviewed these websites to ensure that they are suitable for students. Many websites change frequently, however, and we cannot guarantee that a site's future contents will continue to meet our high standards of quality and educational value. Be advised that students should be closely supervised whenever they access the Internet.

INDEX